Peaceful Mind, Peaceful Life

Conquering Anxiety with Ease

by

Orlando Morales

Contents

Introduction:
Embracing the Anxiety-Free Journey

Anxiety is an uninvited guest that can often make its home in our lives, insidiously weaving its way into the fabric of our daily routines, our sanctuaries, and our minds. For so many, the quest for peace and stillness amidst the noise of modern life is not just a desire but a necessity. We yearn for the serenity that seems just beyond the grasp of our cluttered realities—be it the physical clutter in our homes or the mental clutter in our thoughts.

Within these pages lies a journey—not a quick fix or a magical cure-all, but a pathway trod with intention and understanding. We'll venture through the recesses of our own homes and the complexities of our minds, hand in hand, as we seek to unearth the roots of our anxiety and pave the way for a calmer, more centered existence.

The journey to combat anxiety is one that promises to be as enlightening as it is challenging. Our homes, which should be our sanctuaries, are often inadvertently transformed into breeding grounds for apprehension and stress. Yet, with a little knowledge and a handful of targeted actions, we can transform our living spaces into bastions of tranquility.

In the modern age, our understanding of anxiety extends beyond just the feeling of unease—it's a psychological and physiological phenomenon that demands a well-rounded approach. This book aims to provide just that: an arsenal of strategies, techniques, and habits that together forge the stronghold of a peaceful, anxiety-free home environment.

Emphasizing the importance of awareness, the first chapter dives into recognizing the stew of household stressors simmering beneath the surface. Learning to pinpoint these triggers is the first step towards disarming them. We won't delve into the solutions here—that's a journey reserved for the chapters ahead. Instead, we're setting the stage for understanding the intricate relationship between our environment and our mental states.

Imagine a home that serves as a cocoon, buffering you from the chaos of the outside world—a place where each element fosters a sense of peace and functionality. Chapter two lays the cornerstone for such a sanctuary, not through grand gestures but through simple, practical shifts in how we curate our physical space and honor our daily routines.

Our thoughts, too, need tending. The garden of the mind flourishes with mindfulness techniques sown into the soil of our everyday lives. Chapter three will guide you in implanting mindful practices into your routine so seamlessly, they'll grow to be as natural as breathing.

Clutter isn't just what fills our closets and overflows from our drawers, it is also the mental baggage that weighs us down. In chapter four, we'll explore the freeing practice of decluttering, not just as a chore, but as a liberating art form that clears the mind as much as it does our environments.

A peaceful home isn't solely a result of one's surroundings, but also a product of healthy, nurturing relationships. In chapter five, we will examine the dynamics of our daily interactions and the impact they have on our overall well-being. Communication and support networks are the lifeblood of a harmonious household.

Indeed, the quest for tranquility extends to the very essence of our wellbeing. Chapter six treats the body as the temple that it is, vouching for holistic health practices and dietary habits conducive to a calm mind and a soothed spirit.

No contemporary discussion on well-being would be complete without acknowledging the digital elephant in the room. The double-edged sword of technology plays a pivotal role in our collective anxiety. Chapter seven will tackle this modern dilemma, helping you set boundaries with your devices to reclaim your mental space.

All these components woven together fabricate a tapestry of tranquility for your home, but like any masterpiece, it requires maintenance. The conclusion will empower you to sustain this newly achieved peace, ensuring that once anxiety is banished, it finds no easy path to return.

To walk this path is to embrace change, to unlock the doors of our homes—and hearts—to the possibility of a life less anxious. It is a journey intended to be transformative, instructive, and ultimately, liberating. It's one that recognizes anxiety for what it often is—both an intruder and an informant that signals when our lives are out of balance.

As we journey together through these pages, we're embarking on an exploration—a quest not just for the absence of anxiety, but for the presence of its antithesis: peace, clarity, and a profound sense of home. And so, without further ado, let us step forward, gently but with resolve, into the embrace of an anxiety-free journey.

Chapter 1:
Understanding Anxiety in the Modern Home

As we close the door on our introduction to a journey free from anxiety, let's turn the key to understanding the unique challenges that today's homes face. The modern domestic landscape is often a breeding ground for anxiety, with factors ranging from mounting bills to the never-ending hum of electronic devices contributing to a sense of unrest. Within these walls, the line between work and sanctuary blurs, leaving us in a tenuous balance between relaxation and obligation. However, it's essential to pinpoint the everyday stressors that disrupt our peace before we can begin to address them. In acknowledging the prevalence of these stressors, this chapter lays the groundwork for recognizing the sources of discomfort dwelling in our own living spaces, offering the first step towards reestablishing the home as a haven for calm, rather than a hub of tension. Here, we'll dissect the science behind anxiety, identifying how it manifests within the confines of our walls and preluding the strategies for fostering a serene environment, which we'll explore in the chapters to come.

Recognizing Household Stressors

As we continue on our journey to understand anxiety within the confines of our abodes, it's essential to pinpoint the specific stressors that permeate our domestic environments. Anxiety can seep into our home life through various channels, and identifying these is the first critical step towards creating a sanctuary of peace and tranquility.

Let's begin by considering the physical clutter that often goes unnoticed. It's the pile of mail unattended on the kitchen counter, the toys strewn across the living room floor or the closet that's bursting at the seams. These seemingly innocuous items can subconsciously overwhelm our senses, igniting a sense of chaos that fuels anxiety.

Financial concerns also bring significant stress into the household. The silent pressure of bills, mortgages, or unexpected expenses hangs heavy in the air, often causing sleepless nights and tense family dynamics. Even when not explicitly discussed, financial strain can create a palpable tension felt by all members of the family.

Noise pollution is yet another culprit. Whether it's the constant hum of urban traffic, the neighbor's barking dog, or the cacophony of electronics beeping and buzzing, an excess of noise can heighten our stress response without us even realizing it.

Equally important to consider are the relationships within our homes. Interpersonal conflicts, whether between spouses, siblings, or roommates, can escalate into full-fledged stressors. The ripple effect of a single argument can disrupt the equilibrium of the entire home environment.

Work-related stress doesn't cease at the threshold of our homes. Many of us bring our work home, mentally if not physically. The blur between professional and personal life, especially with the rise of remote working conditions, can introduce a strain that is difficult to shake off.

Our schedules, too, can be sources of stress. Over commitment and the pressure to perform socially, academically, or professionally can spill over into home life, leaving little room for rest and rejuvenation. In our pursuit to do it all, we often neglect the necessity of downtime.

Technology, while an integral part of the modern home, can also contribute to our anxiety. Excessive screen time and the barrage of information and notifications can keep our minds in a constant state of alert, disrupting our home's tranquility.

Moreover, the quest for perfection weighs heavily on many. The societal pressure to maintain an impeccable home, or to be the perfect host, can infuse our living spaces with an undercurrent of anxiety, stripping away the joy of simply being at home.

Lifestyle choices, including diet and physical activity, also play a role. A household that neglects nutritional balance and physical well-being might inadvertently create an environment that is more conducive to stress and less to calmness.

Seasonal changes and weather patterns should not be overlooked either. The lack of sunlight during winter months can lead to a dip in mood levels, affecting the overall atmosphere at home.

Children and pets, though a source of unconditional love, can also contribute to household stress. The constant needs of dependents, from homework help to veterinary visits, add layers of responsibility that can become overwhelming.

Lastly, even our own personal habits can transform into stressors. Procrastination, lack of organization, or poor time management can amplify feelings of anxiety, echoing throughout the household.

Having exposed these various household stressors, it's important to recognize that their existence isn't a sentence to perpetual anxiety. With awareness comes the power to change, to make conscious choices that will steer our homes towards serenity.

We'll explore steps to mitigate the pressures caused by these stressors in the following sections, but for now, let's simply acknowledge their presence. Accepting that these elements influence our mental well-being is fundamental to the process of creating a peaceful home—a refuge that nourishes and supports our journey to an anxiety-free life.

In the next section, "The Science of Anxiety and Its Domestic Triggers," we delve deeper into understanding how and why these stressors affect us. By unraveling the intricacies of our stress responses, we can begin to form a blueprint for an anxiety-resilient home environment. But until then, let's hold onto the awareness that recognizing stressors is a stride towards mastering them, and ultimately, towards achieving an abode that is a haven for our minds and souls.

The Science of Anxiety and Its Domestic Triggers

As we delve deeper into the intricacies of anxiety within the realm of our personal sanctuaries, it's crucial to understand the biological and psychological underpinnings that fuel this condition. Anxiety isn't solely a byproduct of external pressures; it's also rooted in the complex neurochemical landscape of our brains. The experience of feeling anxious involves a series of physiological reactions often described as the "fight or flight" response. At the core, this mechanism serves an evolutionary purpose, preparing our bodies to face threats efficiently.

However, within the modern household, these same biological processes can be activated by stressors that are far from life-threatening. The domestic triggers for anxiety are many and varied, from financial pressures and work responsibilities brought into the home, to relationship dynamics and the perpetual quest for work-life balance. These factors can stimulate our stress hormones like cortisol and adrenaline, leading to an increased state of alertness that, while useful in the short term, can be damaging when sustained.

Understanding these domestic triggers is pivotal, as the home environment should be a refuge, not a breeding ground for stress. For instance, even the layout and design of our homes can inadvertently contribute to unease. Spaces that are cluttered or disorganized can overstimulate the senses, sending subtle cues to our brain that command attention and action, thus exacerbating feelings of anxiety.

The dynamic of the home environment itself is crucial. For parents, persistent worries about children's wellbeing and educational milestones may manifest as an undercurrent of tension. Similarly, the lack of clear boundaries between work and leisure spaces – particularly with the rise of remote working – can prolong the stress associated with professional obligations, making it difficult to find respite in what should be a place of peace.

Even the soundscape of our living spaces can trigger stress responses. The drone of appliances, the perpetual buzz of electronics, or the cacophony emanating from urban surroundings – all can prevent the nervous system from downshifting into a more relaxed state.

It's also worth considering how our sensory experiences within the home can impact our levels of anxiety. Different textures, colors, and lighting can either soothe or stimulate. Bright, harsh lighting may serve well for productivity but can keep our alertness high, while softer, warmer tones encourage relaxation. Similarly, the presence of certain colors in our décor can influence our mood – with cool blues and greens typically having a calming effect, contrasting with vibrant reds and oranges that might raise energy levels.

At a more interpersonal level, the fabric of our home lives can greatly affect our mental state. The communication patterns between household members, whether supportive or strained, play a significant role in determining the emotional tone of our environment. When those interactions are characterized by conflict or misunderstanding, the home can feel less like a sanctuary and more like a source of stress.

Subtler factors may include the expectations we set for ourselves within our personal spaces—whether that's maintaining a perfectly clean home, preparing nutritious meals, or undertaking DIY projects. These self-imposed standards can contribute to a sense of inadequacy or chronic stress, particularly when coupled with the highlight reels of others' lives we often encounter on social media and television.

Moreover, the rituals and routines we establish in our homes can either mitigate or amplify anxiety. Lack of structure may lead to a sense of chaos, while overly rigid schedules can foster a feeling of confinement and pressure. Striking a balance that provides flexibility, yet enough routine to support predictability and a sense of control is critical in reducing domestic anxiety triggers.

Furthermore, the mental load of managing a household—remembering chores, appointments, and social commitments—can weigh heavily on individuals, particularly if that burden is not evenly shared. The cognitive taxation of keeping track of these details is substantial and, without proper management and communication, can increase stress levels significantly.

While it is not possible to eliminate all sources of anxiety, understanding what triggers these sensations and reactions within our home environment is the first step toward more effective management. Discerning these triggers can be a complex endeavor, as they are often interwoven with personal expectations, lifestyle choices, and external pressures.

Much of our ability to counteract these domestic triggers lies in creating an awareness of the underlying causes of anxiety and developing strategies to address them. This involves both short-term solutions to acute stress and long-term changes in our home environment and routines that promote psychological well-being.

Knowledge, as it pertains to anxiety, imparts the power to recognize and reshape our daily domestic patterns. By becoming acquainted with the science of anxiety and its triggers, we fortify ourselves with the tools needed to transform our homes into bastions of calm. This process, however intricate, underlines the foundation of fostering a peaceful and serene living space.

Proactive management of domestic triggers can make a significant difference not only in diminishing the feelings of anxiety but also in enhancing overall quality of life. It allows for a reclamation of the essence of home: a haven of security, comfort, and joy. As we continue to unearth and understand these nuances, we pave the way for a tranquil domestic existence, one that cherishes mental clarity and prioritizes well-being.

Chapter 2:
The Foundation of a Peaceful Home Environment

In the preceding chapter, we've explored the underlying causes of anxiety within the home and how modern life can amplify domestic stressors. Building on that understanding, we now turn to the bedrock upon which serenity is established at home. A tranquil domestic sphere isn't just about what you remove—like tension and chaos—but also about what you purposefully create. It's essential to curate an environment that supports mental clarity and nurtures well-being. This begins with a physical space that's conducive to relaxation—a haven where sights, sounds, and textures interweave to engender peace. Likewise, the syncopation of daily life plays a vital role in our psychological landscape. By setting harmonious routines, family members can navigate the ebb and flow of daily existence with the assurance of stability and predictability that quells anxiety. Bearing in mind the impact of our environment on our mental state, we're poised to delve deeper into the specific strategies that can transform your home into a bastion of tranquility.

Creating a Calming Physical Space

As we transition now to setting the pillars for a serene household, let's concentrate on your environment's tangible aspects. Your surroundings heavily influence your mental state, and a chaotic space often magnifies feelings of unrest. Conversely, a calming physical space can serve as the cornerstone of tranquility in your home.

Consider the senses when creating a soothing atmosphere. Sight plays a crucial role—soft, neutral colors on the walls and decor can have a surprisingly profound effect on your psyche, promoting relaxation and reducing stress. These hues reflect nature's own calming palette, reminding us of the serene simplicity outside our four walls.

Lighting is another critical element. The harshness of overly bright lights can be jarring; instead, opt for warmer, diffused light sources. Lamps with dimmable features and the gentle glow of candles can create a soft ambiance that instantly lowers your heart rate and eases tension.

Uncluttered spaces also contribute to a serene home environment. While we will delve into decluttering strategies later, it's important to note that excessive items on display can overwhelm the mind. Carefully curate your space with only what brings you joy or is necessary, ensuring each item has its place.

Textures around your home affect comfort and tranquility as well. Plush throw pillows, soft blankets, and comfortable seating invite relaxation. These tactile elements can provide a subconscious sense of security and warmth, making it easier to unwind.

Order and symmetry have a surprisingly calming effect, too. When objects are arranged in an ordered fashion, it can provide a sense of balance and control, potentially easing anxiety. This might mean aligning books on a shelf or centering artwork on a wall— simple adjustments that encourage a peaceful environment.

Dedicate an area for relaxation—a nook where you can retreat when you need a mental break. A cozy chair, a stack of your favorite books, and a small table for a cup of tea can become your personal sanctuary within the home.

Our sense of smell can transport us to different moods and memories. Incorporating natural scents through essential oils or scented candles can purify the atmosphere, and certain fragrances like lavender or chamomile are known for their soothing properties.

Nature itself is inherently restful, so a bit of greenery can do wonders. Houseplants not only cleanse the air but also bring a piece of the calming outdoors inside. Even if you're not blessed with a green thumb, low-maintenance plants can flourish and contribute to a more serene living space.

Sound is another dimension of creating a tranquil home environment. Soft background music, the melody of wind chimes, or the gentle bubbling of a small indoor fountain can provide an auditory backdrop that calms the mind and muffles the jarring noise of the outside world.

While technology offers us immense convenience, it also contributes to stress. Consider designating technology-free zones in your home, or areas where screens and gadgets are intentionally absent, to enable true disconnection and relaxation. This practice encourages present-moment awareness and can reduce the everyday strain on your mental well-being.

The way your space flows and functions can be tailored to induce calmness as well. Open walkways and a logical arrangement of furniture can streamline your movements and avoid subliminal frustration. We often underestimate the power of simple navigation in our living spaces on our mental health.

Lastly, personal touches matter. Photos of happy memories or tokens from enjoyable experiences are visual reminders of life's joys and can serve as anchors grounding you in positivity when anxiety tries to take hold.

By methodically cultivating each aspect of your physical surroundings, you usher in an ambiance conducive to mental clarity and peace. Although it may take time to curate your perfect tranquil space, the benefits to your mental health are immeasurable—creating the foundation for an anxiety-free home environment is indeed a pursuit worth every effort.

Remember, what resonates with one person might differ from another, so trust in your intuition. Give yourself permission to experiment with your surroundings, noting how changes make you feel. In time, you'll notice that your space isn't just where you live; it becomes a reflection of the serenity you carry within.

Establishing Harmonious Routines

In our quest towards an anxiety-free home environment, understanding the pivotal role of routines is paramount. Routines can act as the subtle architecture for our daily lives, providing structure and predictability. Moreover, they're capable of fostering a sense of calm, essential for mitigating the chaos that can lead to heightened anxiety.

To begin with, a harmonious routine hinges on consistency. This doesn't mean every minute must be rigorously scheduled—far from it. Rather, it's about establishing reliable anchors throughout your day. Think of routines as a rhythmic dance, where certain steps repeat and create a soothing pattern for the psyche.

Initiate your journey to harmony by contemplating your current rituals. What aspects of your day are already working well for you? It might be your morning coffee, a walk with your dog, or the quiet period right before bed. Recognizing these gems allows you to build around them, rather than starting from scratch.

Now, contemplate the transitions in your day. Can they be smoother? Perhaps mornings feel frantic. An effective routine could involve preparing the next day's essentials the night before thus granting you a more serene start. Simple adjustments in your approach can yield significant benefits.

Harmonious routines also encompass meals. Shared meals can anchor a family's day, offering a moment of connection. Whether it's breakfast or dinner, relaxing into these shared experiences can significantly lower daily stress levels.

When it comes to children, routines are doubly important. They provide a framework that makes children feel secure. A consistent bedtime routine, for example, could significantly lower anxiety levels for both children and parents. As sleep is crucial for mental health, smoothing the path to dreamland each night is a worthy investment.

It's also crucial to weave self-care into your routines. Indulging in a hot bath, or dedicating time to read a book can be highly beneficial. These acts can serve as personal rituals to signal to your mind that it's time to slow down and recharge, which goes a long way in nurturing your mental wellbeing.

The incorporation of physical activity can't be overlooked either. Regular exercise, whether it's yoga in your living room, a gym session, or a brisk walk in the park, should be slotted into your routine to release tension and increase endorphins, the body's natural stress relievers.

Implementing these routines into your life might initially require conscious effort. But it's imperative to remember that flexibility should remain a core component. There's no need to impose rigid structures that could inadvertently create more stress. Instead, opt for routines that are robust enough to withstand minor disruptions.

Equally important is adapting your routines to seasonal changes. As daylight and weather patterns shift, so too may your ideal routine. Embracing these natural cycles can bring about a deeper connection to time and place, grounding you further in the present moment, which is inherently calming.

In addition, consider your routines as they relate to work and personal time especially if you work from home. Establishing clear boundaries between the two can prevent work stress from seeping into your family life. The transition from one to the other can be signaled by a specific routine, like changing your attire or taking a short walk, to mentally shift gears.

For many, evenings can be a source of stress as the mind replays the day's events. A harmonious nightly routine, perhaps involving meditation or gentle stretching, can serve as a cue to your body and mind that it's time to wind down and release the day's burdens.

Finally, it's key to review your routines periodically. Life changes, and so should your routines. Regularly revisiting them ensures they evolve to meet your current needs and continue to serve their purpose as custodians of your peace.

Establishing harmonious routines is an investment in your home's tranquility and your mental clarity. These routines operate almost like a soft melody in the background of your life, a lullaby that can soothe frayed nerves and encourage a more mindful, peaceful existence. Allow yourself the grace to experiment, adjust, and find the rhythm that resonates best with you and your household.

In the next chapter, we will delve into mindfulness techniques. But until then, allow the foundational routines you're building to

begin their work of transforming your home into the serene
sanctuary   you   seek.

Chapter 3:
Mindfulness Techniques for the Home

As we step through the threshold of creating a serene environment, let's infuse our newfound calm with mindfulness techniques designed specifically for the home. Picture your living space as a sanctuary where every breath ushers in tranquility and each moment is an opportunity for presence. Mindfulness—being fully engaged with the present, aware of where we are and what we're doing—isn't just a solitary practice; it's a daily commitment that casts a gentle yet transformative glow on mundane tasks, converting them into rituals of peace. By integrating simple practices like mindful meditation and focused breathing, we can anchor our thoughts and find stillness amidst the hustle of home life. It isn't just about sitting in silence; it's about awakening to the subtle rhythm of our domestic dance and allowing the familiar to reveal its own quiet beauty. Urging calm in the midst of chaos, these techniques are more than mere exercises; they're a loving embrace for the mind, ensuring every corner of our abode breathes with intent and every action reflects the harmony we seek.

Practicing Mindful Meditation and Breathing

As we delve into the transformative power of Mindful Meditation and Breathing, let's remember that these practices can serve as a sanctuary amidst the whir of daily life. Imagine infusing each breath with serenity, consciously drawing in calm and exhaling the commotion that grips the mind. Visualize cultivating a serene mental garden where each meditation session nurtures the soul's flora with tranquility. It starts simply: dedicate a quiet corner of your home for this venture—a cushion, a gentle hint of sunlight, perhaps a soothing scent. Here, seated or reclined, embarking on a rhythmic breathing journey, we'll navigate through the internal tides. With each in-breath, count calmly to four, hold for a beat of peace, then gracefully release to a count of six. It's a dance, a gentle ebb and flow of inhalation and exhalation, where mindfulness anchors you to the present. Let each diaphragmatic breath be a whisper, telling stress it has no home in your chest. With consistent practice, these sacred moments of mindful breathing become a fortress of tranquility, safeguarding you from life's tempests.

Incorporating Mindfulness into Daily Tasks offers a remarkable transformation for individuals seeking mental clarity and reduction of anxiety. As one emerges from understanding the science of anxiety and recognizing household stressors, it is vital to seamlessly weave mindfulness into the very fabric of everyday activities. Mindfulness, the practice of being fully present and engaged in the moment, devoid of judgment and overthinking, can be an antidote to anxiety's disquiet.

Let's begin with morning rituals. These are moments that can easily slip into autopilot, but they present a perfect opportunity to practice mindfulness. Rather than racing through your grooming routine, slow down. Feel the bristles of the toothbrush against your gums, the temperature of the water as you wash your face, and the texture of the towel as you dry off. Each sensation is a call to the present moment, a reminder that you are here, now.

Tending to household chores can also become mindful acts. For example, when doing the dishes, notice the sensation of the soap bubbles on your skin, the clink sound of dishes, the rhythmic motion of scrubbing. By focusing on these details, you cultivate a meditative state that brings calmness, pushing aside worries and stresses.

Even the simple act of preparing a meal is an opportunity for mindfulness. Engage all your senses as you chop vegetables, feeling the knife slice through each piece. Note the colours on your cutting board, the sizzle sound as food hits the pan, and the aromas wafting up. Cooking thus becomes not just a task but a multisensory experience, keeping you anchored to the moment.

At your workstation or during professional endeavors, mindfulness can enhance focus and productivity. Before starting a task, take a few deep breaths and set an intention for what you're about to do. As you work, remain aware of your posture, the feeling of your fingers typing, and the mental processes as you solve problems or create. These moments of awareness can serve as a grounding technique, keeping you centered amidst a bustling work environment.

Mindfulness doesn't shy away from the mundane either. Take, for instance, the act of waiting—be it in line or in traffic. This can easily become a wellspring for irritation or mindless scrolling on a phone. Instead, view these pauses in your day as a chance to check in with yourself. Observe your breath, the tensions in your body, your thoughts. Simply observe without trying to change anything; it is a practice of awareness and acceptance.

Interaction with technology, while often inevitable, should not become a mindless extension of the self. When checking emails or engaging in social media, do so with full awareness. Set time limits and intentions. Knowing why you are engaging with these platforms helps maintain a purposeful relationship with technology, rather than falling victim to the infinite scroll and the anxiety that it can provoke.

The art of conversation, too, should be touched by mindfulness. Listen actively when speaking with family members. Notice their expressions, tone, and body language. Fully engaging in discussions not only strengthens relationships but also helps you remain in the present, away from the pull of past regrets and future concerns.

Physical exercise, often seen as a task to improve health, can also be approached mindfully. Whether you're stretching, walking, or lifting weights, focus on your breath and the movement of your muscles. This integration of mindfulness and physical activity can turn routine exercise into a dual action of strengthening both body and mind.

Your evening wind-down routine is equally ripe for mindfulness practice. As you prepare for bed, reflect on the day with gratitude for the moments you were present. Contemplate how mindfulness has made each task richer and more meaningful. Allow these thoughts to lead you into a peaceful night's sleep, free from the chaos of unchecked thoughts.

To ensure mindfulness becomes a habit in daily tasks, consider setting reminders throughout the day. This could be a simple note placed in common areas of the home or a small chime on a phone or watch. These prompts can gently nudge you back to the present moment, encouraging continuous practice.

It's important to approach mindfulness with patience and kindness towards oneself. It's not about perfection or a constant state of Zen. It is normal for the mind to wander; the practice is in the return, each time guiding your attention back to the task at hand with compassion and without self-judgment.

As we engage in this process, mindfulness transforms from a series of exercises into a way of being. You'll start to notice a natural presence in each activity without exertion. Anxiety becomes less gripping as your mind learns to stay with what is happening rather than getting entangled in what might happen.

Implementing mindfulness into daily tasks is not a one-size-fits-all process. Personalize your mindfulness journey to fit your lifestyle and preferences. Whether it be through a dedicated practice like meditation or the mindful execution of routine tasks, the goal is to cultivate a state of awareness that permeates your every action, fostering mental tranquility.

Incorporating mindfulness into your daily life demands consistent practice, but it's within this dedication that peace and mental clarity are found. By savoring the moment, appreciating small tasks, and returning to the now, you build a powerful defense against the tendrils of anxiety, creating an environment of serenity in both your home and mind.

Chapter 4:
The Art of Decluttering for Mental Clarity

As we journey further into the heart of an anxiety-free home, we encounter the transformative space of Chapter 4: "The Art of Decluttering for Mental Clarity." A cluttered environment can cloud the mind and trigger stress, often unbeknownst to us. Herein, we'll explore how the intentional act of removing excess from our surroundings is not just a physical process, but a mental expedition that can lead to unmistakable serenity. We'll dive into the subtle yet profound connection between the items we choose to keep around us and the inner peace we yearn to achieve. But remember, decluttering isn't just about throwing things out—it's about curating your personal space in a way that reflects and nurtures your mental state, ensuring that every object in your haven has a purpose and contributes positively to your mental landscape. This chapter serves as a gateway, opening the door to decluttering techniques that not only clear out physical messes but also pave the way for a rejuvenated mind, free from the anchors of the unnecessary.

The KonMari Method and Anxiety Reduction

Continuing our exploration into the art of decluttering for mental clarity, it's essential to understand the unique process that has captured the attention of millions seeking a more serene environment: the KonMari Method. Developed by Marie Kondo, a Japanese organizing consultant, this method isn't just about tidying up; it's an intricate dance with your belongings that allows you to harmonize with your living space. Its fundamental principle is simple yet profound: if an item doesn't spark joy, it has no place in your life.

The act of decluttering itself can be a source of anxiety for many. Staring at piles of forgotten clothes, papers we meant to file away, gifts from loved ones we never used, can all contribute to a sensation of overwhelming stress. The KonMari Method approaches this chaos with a calming strategy that systematically reduces the clutter, and correspondingly, the anxiety associated with it.

How does one start this journey? Through the act of categorizing. Marie Kondo suggests tidying by category, not by location. This approach ensures you confront each class of item across your entire living space, one at a time, which prevents the common cycle of decluttering one area only to shift the clutter to another. In focusing on categories, you're directed to take each step with mindfulness and intention.

Beginning with clothing - often the least emotionally loaded category - you pile every piece you own in one place. This mountain of fabric is not just a pile; it's a mirror reflecting back your purchasing habits, your changes in taste, and perhaps most importantly, your capacity to let go. With each piece of clothing you hold, you're tasked to ask, "Does this spark joy?" Not "Will I wear this someday?" or "I wore this once," but a simple, immediate connection to joy.

The beauty of this method lies in its capacity to turn decluttering into a self-discovery ritual. The KonMari Method encourages you to trust your intuition about what brings you happiness. Through this, it becomes a therapeutic tool for understanding and setting your priorities and values, which is a significant step in alleviating anxiety.

As you proceed through categories – books, papers, komono (miscellaneous items), and sentimental items – you exercise your decision-making skills. This effectuates a powerful sense of control and completion which can be cathartic for those who have felt paralyzed by their clutter for years. The completion of each category provides a tangible result that further motivates and decreases anxiety.

The process of thanking items that do not spark joy before discarding them is another unique aspect of the KonMari Method. It provides a moment of closure and gratitude, allowing a respectful release of belongings. This step curbs feelings of guilt and helps lift the mental burden that often comes with letting go of possessions.

By fostering a disciplined mind capable of identifying joy, the KonMari Method extends its benefits beyond your immediate surroundings. It equips you with a discerning mental framework that applies to other areas of life, reducing anxiety by clarifying which tasks, relationships, and activities truly enrich your existence.

Visual clarity is a by-product of this method - a clear space mirrors a clear mind. The physical act of decluttering can often kickstart a deeper mental decluttering, helping to sift through the cognitive clutter of everyday anxieties and stressors.

The order and structure that emerge from a KonMari-organized home speak to a psychological need for predictability and organization, which anxiety often disrupts. With each item in its right place, the predictability of your environment can improve overall mood and mental clarity.

Additionally, the concept of filling your space exclusively with items that spark joy essentially turns your home into a sanctuary of positivity. This positivity becomes a buffer against the negative thoughts and worries that can trigger anxiety, fostering a more peaceful and joyous daily life.

It's important to recognize that the decluttering process itself can momentarily increase anxiety levels. But the KonMari Method provides a structured approach to manage and channel that anxiety into productive actions, ensuring that the ritualistic nature of the method becomes a comforting practice rather than a daunting task.

Through this method, one not only transforms their living space but also adopts a philosophy that enhances daily life. Decisions become easier; habits align with personal values, and a sense of serenity in your environment supports a peaceful state of mind.

The KonMari Method isn't just about minimizing possessions or organizing drawers. It is a comprehensive campaign for redefining your relationship with the material world and consequently, with your inner world. As you align your belongings with your joy, you streamlines your thoughts, reduce your anxiety, and pave the way for enduring mental clarity.

By inviting the KonMari Method into your life, you're not simply tidying up – you're setting the stage for a more mindful, joyful, and tranquil existence. This clarity resonates beyond your shelves and closets, touching every facet of your life with the gentle reminder that joy is indeed, the ultimate criterion for a life well-lived, and a mind well-settled.

Sustainable Habits for a Clutter-Free Home

Embarking on a mission to declutter is not just a one-time effort; it's the beginning of adopting a lifestyle that persistently favors simplicity and order. Minimizing the clutter in your space is synonymous with minimizing the chaos in your mind. A clear space reflects a clear mind, and maintaining such an environment requires the cultivation of sustainable habits. Let's explore how you can embrace these practices to keep your home—and your mind—clutter-free.

Maintaining a clutter-free home starts with mindful acquisition. Before you bring an item into your living space, ask yourself if it serves a genuine need or brings you joy. If the answer is "no," consider skipping the purchase. By being selective about what we allow into our homes, we reduce the potential for clutter to accumulate over time.

The key to sustaining a decluttered home is to ensure that everything has a place. When every item has a designated spot, it becomes easier to return things after using them. This habit also simplifies the cleaning process, making it far less overwhelming to keep on top of household organization.

Incorporating the habit of regular 'mini-decluttering' sessions is tremendously effective. Instead of letting things pile up, taking ten minutes daily to tidy up a particular area can make a big difference. Whether it's sorting through mail, clearing up a drawer, or arranging the shoes in your closet, these short bursts of decluttering prevent the buildup of disarray.

Adopting a "one-in, one-out" rule can significantly help maintain decluttered spaces. For every new item that enters your home, commit to letting go of something else. This balance ensures that your possessions don't expand beyond the space you've allotted for them, keeping your environment spacious and serene.

It's also essential to avoid the temptation of the "just in case" mindset. Keeping items because we think they might be useful someday can lead to excess clutter. Instead, trust that you can acquire or borrow what you need, when you need it. This mindset fosters a sense of freedom and ensures your space only contains what is truly necessary.

Furthermore, digital clutter can be as suffocating to your mental clarity as physical clutter. Regularly detox your digital space by organizing files, deleting unnecessary emails, and unsubscribing from unwanted newsletters. A clean digital environment helps reduce anxiety and enhances your ability to focus.

Embracing sustainability in your home doesn't just mean reducing waste—it also means making the most of what you have. Repairing and repurposing items not only extends their life but also prevents the environmental and clutter impact of continually buying new. Become an advocate for a lifestyle that cherishes and creatively reimagines the belongings you already own.

To keep surfaces clear, implement a "no-dump" policy. Kitchen counters, dining tables, and other surfaces are often magnets for random items. Make it a rule that these areas are not drop zones for mail, keys, or other miscellanea. Having a specific place for these items prevents them from consuming your space.

Educate yourself about the life cycle of your possessions. When you understand the resources and energy that go into making the items you buy, you become more aware of the impact of your consumption. This awareness can inspire you to keep purchases to a minimum and to dispose of items responsibly when they're no longer needed.

Organizing your items vertically can save considerable space. Use shelves, hooks, and vertical organizers to keep your belongings orderly. This method keeps your floorspace open and airy, contributing to a sense of calm and openness in your home.

Seasonal decluttering can align your living space with your state of being throughout the year. As seasons change, so do our activities and needs. By adjusting your environment accordingly, you maintain physical and mental space for the present moment, rather than clinging to what's no longer current or necessary.

Involve household members in the decluttering process. When everyone takes responsibility for maintaining a clutter-free space, it becomes far easier to keep a harmonious home environment. Establishing decluttering as a shared value creates a collective investment in the tranquility of your living space.

Reward yourself for maintaining a decluttered home. Acknowledging your efforts reinforces positive behavior. Treat yourself to a pleasant activity or experience—not more stuff—as a way to celebrate the peaceful environment you've cultivated. This serves as motivation to keep up the good habits.

Remember, the goal is not to create a stark or sterile environment, but one that feels peaceful and nurturing to you. Our surroundings have a profound influence on our mental state, and by curating a clutter-free home, we nurture a sense of clarity and calmness within ourselves. Practice these sustainable habits consistently, and you'll find that both your home and your mind remain serene sanctuaries amidst the bustle of everyday life.

Chapter 5:
Nurturing Relationships, Nurturing Peace

In the wake of decluttering both our physical spaces and our minds, we must recognize that the cornerstone of continued tranquility lies within the realm of our relationships. When we establish a strong foundation of communication and support within our homes, we're not just contributing to our personal well-being but cultivating an environment ripe for peace to flourish. It's through the delicate process of consistently nurturing our bonds—being attentive to the needs of those we live with and expressing our own in ways that build, rather than erode, mutual respect—that our home transforms into a sanctuary. This chapter aims to guide us in fortifying these connections, for it's in the heartwarming embrace of understanding and collaboration that one finds a powerful antidote to anxiety's pervasive whisper.

Communicating Effectively with Household Members

Effective communication is the cement that holds the family structure together. Creating an environment of open dialogue within the home is not just about speaking and being heard; it's about understanding and nurturing relationships. To alleviate anxiety and foster peace, developing a keen sense for communicating thoughts, needs, and emotions is paramount among household members.

Starting with active listening, it's important to give full attention to the speaker, take note of their body language, and reflect back what you've understood. This isn't just about nodding in agreement, but truly engaging with what's being said, asking clarifying questions, and demonstrating empathy. This practice encourages trust and dissipates tension, setting a tone of respect and care.

Nonviolent communication is another cornerstone. It emphasizes expressing oneself without blame or judgment, focusing on one's own feelings and needs rather than accusing others. For example, saying "I feel overwhelmed when the living room is messy, and I need a calm space to relax" is more constructive than "You never clean up after yourself."

Timing can be everything when it comes to heart-to-heart conversations. Bringing up an important topic when everyone is relaxed and free from distractions is usually more productive than during a stressful moment. Remember, it's about making communication less about confrontation and more about connection.

It's vital to adapt the way we communicate according to the age and understanding of the individuals we live with. Children, for example, may need more visual cues and concrete examples, whereas teenagers may require a more collaborative approach, ensuring they feel heard and their opinions valued. On the other hand, communication with a partner or elder family members may necessitate a deeper level of emotional intelligence.

Clear boundaries are imperative. They establish guidelines on what is acceptable behavior within the home. When communicated assertively, everyone understands the limits, which helps to reduce uncertainties and anxiety stemming from the unknown or unspoken expectations.

Conflict resolution skills should be honed within the household. Disagreements are natural, but approaching them with a solution-oriented mindset can shift the focus from problem to resolution.

Collaborative strategies, like brainstorming solutions together, can lead to more harmonious outcomes.

Emotional expression shouldn't be taboo. Encouraging household members to share their feelings, whether through verbal communication, art, or another medium, is therapeutic. It contributes to mental clarity by allowing release in a safe environment, thwarting the build-up of internal angst.

The dissemination of responsibilities and tasks must also be communicated effectively. By ensuring that everyone understands their roles within the household, ambiguity can be minimized, resulting in a smoother daily operation that's less likely to induce stress and anxiety.

Appreciation and positive reinforcement play a major role in enhancing the emotional climate of the home. By verbally acknowledging each other's contributions and efforts, a culture of gratitude is cultivated. This not only reinforces positive behavior but elevates the overall mood.

Feedback and constructive criticism, when approached with care, can pave the way for growth and improvement. This must be done with a focus on the behavior rather than the person, such as saying, "Can we find a way to keep track of who does what chore?" instead of "You're not doing enough around the house."

It's important to create spaces within the home for individual expression. Just as communal areas benefit from group interaction, personal spaces allow for introspection and self-communication. Balancing shared and personal environments contributes to everyone's mental clarity.

Lastly, never underestimate the power of humor. Light-hearted communication can diffuse tension and inject joy into daily interactions, which in turn can alleviate feelings of anxiety.

In conclusion, good communication within the household isn't just an art; it's a critical building block for maintaining an anxiety-free living space. By actively listening, expressing needs without blame, resolving conflicts with a collaborative spirit, and balancing individual and communal needs, household members pave the way toward nurturing relationships and nurturing peace.

Remember, each interaction is an opportunity to strengthen bonds and build a more tranquil home life. By focusing on effective communication, families are well on their way to transforming their shared spaces into havens of comfort, understanding, and mutual support.

Building Support Networks Within the Home

As we transition from understanding individual stressors and mastering personal calm, let's focus on strengthening the fabric that holds our domestic life together—the support network within our home. Constructing robust support systems amongst family members and housemates isn't just about chore distribution or shared calendars; it's about weaving a web of emotional, mental, and practical backing that can act as a safety net in times of stress and anxiety.

A foundational aspect of these networks is open communication. It's essential to form a habit of discussing emotions and concerns regularly. Foster an environment where expressing vulnerability isn't seen as a weakness but as a vital step towards deeper connections and mutual understanding. Through this openness, individuals feel heard and supported, reducing the internal pressure that can accumulate and lead to anxiety.

But communication alone isn't enough. Active listening is a skill that requires development and practice. A true support network within the home thrives when members not only share but also deeply understand each other's experiences. This takes patience and empathy, as we often need to set aside our own immediate reactions and focus purely on the speaker's perspective.

Within these conversations, it's important to set boundaries. Every person has limits regarding what they can offer emotionally or practically. By acknowledging and respecting these limits, we avoid overburdening individuals, which in turn can lead to resentment or burnout. A support network should empower, not incapacitate.

The diversity of support is another pillar. It's unrealistic to expect a single person to fulfill all support roles. Spread the load by identifying different strengths and capabilities within the household. One person may be an excellent listener, while another could be more adept at providing pragmatic solutions. Each role is valuable and needed.

Team-building activities can fortify these connections. Whether it's a family game night or a shared meal prep session, engaging in activities together deepens bonds and creates a safety mechanism for when tension arises. It gives a sense of belonging and togetherness that is stronger than any individual anxiety.

Conflict resolution skills are indispensable in a support network. Home should be a refuge, but even the closest-knit families face conflicts. The ability to navigate disagreements with respect and without escalation can prevent a whole host of anxiety-inducing situations. This can be taught and practiced so that when conflicts do arise, they are dealt with constructively.

Let's not forget the role of children in the support network. Encouraging children to participate, according to their age and ability, fosters a sense of responsibility and pride in contributing to the family's well-being. This also sets a precedent for them to seek and offer support throughout their lives.

For adults in the home, actively working on relationships is key. This can mean date nights for partners, one-on-one outings with friends or relatives, or even small daily gestures that show care and appreciation. Strong adult relationships often set the tone for the overall emotional climate of the home.

It's also wise to include external support when necessary. Friends, extended family, or mental health professionals can offer fresh perspectives and specialized help that family members might not be equipped to provide. They can be a critical part of the larger support network.

Remember that support networks are not static; they need regular maintenance and adjustment. Life changes, such as a new job, moving house, or personal growth, can shift the dynamics of support needs. Regular check-ins help ensure that the support network adapts to these changes.

Encouraging autonomy within the network plays a dual role. When individuals know how to manage their stress and assert their needs, it relieves pressure on others and simultaneously enriches the overall support system by modeling self-reliance and self-care. This balance between independence and interdependence should be celebrated and encouraged.

Lastly, gratitude goes a long way. A culture of thanking and appreciating each other's contributions, no matter how small, can cement the bonds within the support network. A simple 'thank you' can transform an obligatory task into a recognized gift of service.

In essence, a support network should be the living, breathing heart of the home—a system as complex and dynamic as the individuals within it. With careful attention and tender upkeep, this network transforms a mere living space into a sanctuary where relationships flourish and peace is not just a concept, but a practiced reality.

As we encapsulate the essence of building these vital support networks within the home, remember that the journey to nurturing relationships and nurturing peace is ongoing and ever-evolving. This network is not only a tool to reduce anxiety but is also a testament to the strength of unity and the resilience that comes from solidarity and compassion within our most intimate social constructs—the home.

Chapter 6:
Holistic Health at Home

With a firm groundwork of understanding anxiety and exploring the various methods for cultivating tranquility within the household, it's essential to now turn our focus towards the embodiment of holistic health practices that empower us to sustain an anxiety-free living space. Enveloping oneself in an environment that nurtures every aspect of your well-being is key to fostering mental clarity and stability. Embracing holistic health isn't simply about occasional practices; it demands a consistent and inclusive approach that infuses calm into every quarter of your home life. By integrating natural elements into your daily routine and paying heed to the sustenance that fuels both body and mind, you create a resilient buffer against stress. The sanctuary of your home becomes a testament to balance and rejuvenation, ensuring that each breath and each bite taken within its walls contributes to a serene and refreshed state of mind. In this pivotal chapter, we delve into the seamless integration of all-encompassing health strategies into your living spaces, transforming them into bastions of peace that support and echo your journey towards permanent anxiety relief.

Embracing Natural Remedies and Aromatherapy

The pursuit of a serene and stress-free existence at home isn't confined to the physical or the visible; it extends into the realm of scents and natural elixirs that can influence our mental state. By integrating natural remedies and aromatherapy into our daily lives, we pave the way for a holistic approach to combating anxiety and fostering mental clarity.

Essential oils, the heart of aromatherapy, are extracted from plants and capture their scents and therapeutic properties. These oils can profoundly influence our limbic system, the part of the brain responsible for emotions and memories. When diffused into the air or applied topically, they can induce relaxation, improve mood, or even enhance concentration.

Consider lavender, whose purple blooms don't just charm the eye but also provide one of the most versatile essential oils. Its floral scent is associated with relaxation and is often used to alleviate stress, promote a restful night's sleep, and reduce feelings of anxiety. Simply adding a few drops to a diffuser or a warm bath can invoke a sense of calm throughout your home environment.

But the world of aromatherapy doesn't stop at lavender. Each essential oil holds its unique benefits. For instance, lemon oil can uplift mood, peppermint can stimulate the mind, and eucalyptus can clear the nasal passages, enhancing overall respiration and well-being.

A key to successfully employing these scents is understanding how to blend them. Like a symphony, where each instrument plays its part, different oils can be combined to create a harmonious blend that's tailored to your home's needs. A mix of rosemary, lemon, and peppermint, for example, can invigorate the senses and help maintain focus during busy days.

Aside from diffusing, topical application mixed with a carrier oil, like almond or coconut oil, allows these essences to soothe the skin and penetrate the body to provide their therapeutic effects. A gentle massage with these oils can reduce stress and tension, but remember, it's always recommended to perform a patch test to ensure there are no allergic reactions.

Aside from essential oils, other natural remedies hold a place of honor in the home apothecary. Herbal teas, for instance, are a testament to the gentle power of nature. Chamomile, with its mild apple-like taste, can soothe nerves and is an excellent beverage to enjoy before bedtime. On the other hand, green tea contains L-Theanine, an amino acid that promotes relaxation without drowsiness.

Herbs can also be utilized in their dried form. Sachets filled with dried lavender flowers, placed in drawers or under pillows, serve as a passive aromatherapy tool, continuously releasing a subtle scent. These dried bouquets are also a visually pleasing way to bring nature's tranquility into your home.

But embracing these remedies and aromas goes beyond just their selection and use; it's about creating a ritual that signals to your mind and body that it's time to unwind and rejuvenate. Perhaps it's the act of lighting a scented candle before meditation or the evening preparation of an herbal tonic; these routines can serve as a foundation for lasting peace and clarity.

Integration into daily life is key. Maybe it starts with a single oil or plant but grows into a thoughtfully curated collection that addresses various aspects of wellness. The beauty of natural remedies and aromatherapy is their versatility and adaptability to personal needs and preferences.

It's also important to note that quality matters. With the growing popularity of essential oils and natural remedies, so too have concerns about purity and sustainability. Opt for quality, pure, and ethically sourced products to ensure the best outcomes for your health and the planet.

In your journey towards an anxiety-free and mentally clear state, remember that balance is crucial. These natural wonders are potent, and their usage should be respectful of their strength. Adhering to recommended doses and methods of application will ensure you reap the benefits without adverse effects.

Within your home, consider designating spaces for aromatherapy. A small corner with a diffuser, a shelf of neatly organised oils, or a nook for your evening tea ritual; these physical enclaves of calm can anchor your commitment to a holistic and harmonious lifestyle.

Lastly, incorporate educational moments. As you explore various remedies and fragrances, take the time to learn about their origins, cultural uses, and specific benefits. This not only deepens your appreciation but also surrounds you with a narrative of wellness and healing.

In the embrace of natural remedies and aromatherapy, we find an age-old wisdom deftly woven into the modern fabric of an anxiety-conscious home. These practices, distilled from the very essence of nature, hold the keys to unlocking a peaceful, clear-minded existence amidst the cacophony of daily life.

Healthy Eating for a Calm Mind

Nourishing the body with the right foods can be a powerful tool for calming the mind and maintaining mental clarity. In the labyrinth of stress management strategies, diet often serves as an anchor, steadying us amidst the waves of anxiety that can disrupt daily life. Our previous chapters have laid the groundwork for a serene home environment, and now it's time to explore how dietary choices can complement these efforts and help mitigate anxiety.

The relationship between food and mood is complex but undeniable. Serotonin, a neurotransmitter often referred to as the happiness chemical, has a significant part of its production occurring in our gut. Thus, a balanced diet directly affects our emotional state, impacting how we handle stress and anxiety. When we nourish our gut with whole, nutrient-rich foods, we are essentially fortifying our minds against the onslaught of stressors.

Starting with the basics, hydration plays a pivotal role in our mental wellness. Drinking adequate water throughout the day helps to maintain the balance of body fluids, which includes digestion, absorption, and even cognitive functions. Dehydration has been linked to increased feelings of anxiety, so it's essential to keep sipping water, herbal teas, or infused hydrating options to support a serene state of mind.

Complex carbohydrates are your allies in the quest for an anxiety-free existence. Unlike simple sugars, which can cause a spike and crash in blood sugar levels, complex carbs release glucose gradually. They fuel the brain consistently and help regulate mood. Foods such as oats, quinoa, brown rice, and sweet potatoes are excellent choices for sustained energy and mental clarity.

Don't underestimate the power of omega-3 fatty acids either. Found in foods like salmon, flaxseeds, and walnuts, these essential fats are linked to cognitive function and emotional health. Incorporating sources of omega-3s into your diet may help alleviate symptoms of anxiety and depression by supporting brain health and reducing inflammation.

Lean proteins are another cornerstone of a diet aimed at reducing anxiety. They provide amino acids, which are the building blocks for neurotransmitters like serotonin and dopamine that regulate mood. By including a moderate amount of high-quality proteins such as poultry, tofu, eggs, and legumes in your meals, you're supporting your brain's ability to cope with stress.

Antioxidant-rich foods, including dark leafy greens, berries, and nuts, combat oxidative stress, a biological process linked with anxiety. By neutralizing free radicals, antioxidants protect the brain from damage and support overall mental health. Make these foods a staple to benefit from their protective qualities.

Magnesium is an often overlooked mineral that can play a significant role in managing anxiety. It's involved in over 300 biochemical reactions in the body, and a deficiency can lead to heightened stress and anxiety levels. Incorporate magnesium-rich foods like spinach, pumpkin seeds, and yogurt into your diet to harness their calming effects.

Probiotics found in yogurt, kefir, and fermented foods like sauerkraut support the gut-brain axis. A healthy gut microbiome is associated with a lower risk of anxiety, as the balance of bacteria in our digestive system can influence the production and regulation of mood-regulating neurotransmitters.

Vitamin B complex, particularly B12 and folate (B9), are crucial for maintaining optimal brain health and managing stress. They are vital for the production of serotonin and dopamine, and deficiencies can be linked to increased anxiety. Look to sources such as eggs, dairy products, leafy greens, and legumes to make sure you're getting enough of these important vitamins.

Harnessing the subtle powers of herbs can also contribute to a calm mind. Herbal teas such as chamomile, lavender, and lemon balm are known for their natural soothing properties. Incorporating these into your evening routine may lead to better sleep and less anxiety the next day.

While focusing on what to include in your diet, it's also important to note what to limit. High intake of caffeine and alcohol can exacerbate anxiety, disrupting sleep and mood. Modifying your consumption of these substances can have a profound impact on your mental state, providing a more stable foundation for your overall well-being.

It's worth noting that the journey to an anxiety-free life isn't about strict dietary restrictions; it's about balance and moderation. Listening to your body and understanding how it reacts to different foods will guide you toward a diet that supports your mental health.

Meal planning and preparation can be an act of mindfulness in itself, and the intentionality behind selecting and cooking food can reinforce your commitment to mental clarity. Stepping into the kitchen becomes a therapeutic ritual, where you have the opportunity to create nourishing meals that feed both your body and mind.

As you integrate these nutritional principles into your life, remember that healthy eating is not a panacea but a vital piece of the puzzle. It's an investment in your long-term emotional well-being and a testament to the power of self-care. By choosing foods that foster a calm mind, you are laying yet another brick in the foundation of your tranquil home environment, one meal at a time.

Chapter 7:
Technology and Anxiety

In our quest to create a sanctuary of serenity, we've meticulously crafted domestic realms that cater to our mental well-being. We've inhaled the fragrance of lavender through aromatherapy and forged familial bonds that serve as a bastion against unease. Yet, as we journey onward, we encounter the double-edged sword that is technology. It's woven into the very fabric of our existence, promising connection and convenience while simultaneously sowing seeds of restlessness. In this chapter, we'll navigate the tumultuous digital landscape to find balance. We'll delve into strategies for managing our interactions with screens, ensuring that they serve as tools for productivity, not perpetuators of panic. It's about making intentional choices—like establishing tech-free zones in our homes—to reclaim our mental space and cultivate an atmosphere where calm can flourish. Our homes, after all, should be refuges, not repositories of digital noise. So let's examine how we can judiciously utilize technology to enhance, not encroach, our quest for tranquility and mental clarity.

Balancing Screen Time and Mental Wellness

As we navigate the intricate relationship between technology and anxiety, it becomes clear that moderating our screen time is crucial for mental wellness. The luminous glow of our devices often keeps us tethered to the stressors of the digital world, inhibiting the serenity we strive for in our abodes. Insights from psychological studies suggest that intentional disconnection can rejuvenate the mind, reducing anxiety and increasing present-moment awareness. Achieving this balance involves setting clear boundaries for device usage, engaging in enriching activities that occupy our hands and minds, and savoring the natural environment around us. By recognizing the imperceptible but potent impact that relentless screen engagement can have on our stress levels, we can craft a strategy to integrate technology into our lives in a way that supports rather than detracts from our mental tranquility. Establishing this equilibrium means not only limiting the duration of our digital interactions but also being mindful of content consumption, ensuring our screen time works to promote feelings of calm and connection rather than exacerbating anxieties.

Creating Tech-Free Zones and Routines is an integral step towards crafting an abode bathed in tranquility. We live in an age where digital devices are omnipresent, and while they offer remarkable conveniences, their persistent use can contribute significantly to anxiety and stress. Establishing spaces and practices within the home devoid of technology's buzz and glare can have profound effects on mental clarity and stress reduction.

To begin, let's identify the main culprits that intertwine our daily lives with technology—smartphones, computers, tablets, and televisions are the most common. They keep us constantly connected to the outside world, often at the expense of neglecting our inner peace. The goal here is not to vilify these devices but to manage their place in our lives to provide balance.

First, designate specific zones in your home as tech-free. These should be areas conducive to relaxation, conversation, and reflection. The bedroom is an excellent place to start. By removing televisions, computers, and charging stations from where you sleep, you encourage the mind to unwind and prepare for rest. It's a bold step, but one that firmly roots the bedroom as a sanctuary for rest.

Another impactful zone is the dining area. Encouraging technology-free meals fosters deeper connections with those around your table. Engaging in uninterrupted conversation allows for a sharing of thoughts and emotions, free from digital distractions. This practice nurtures relationships and eases the mind from the day's barrage of information.

Creating routines around these tech-free zones is equally as important as selecting the right areas. For example, establishing a morning ritual without reaching for your phone upon waking sets a peaceful tone for the day. Take those first moments of wakefulness to stretch, meditate, or reflect, without the influence of electronics.

Similarly, an evening routine might involve reading, journaling, or simply conversing with loved ones. At least an hour before bedtime, disconnect from all devices to signal your mind that it's time to wind down. This practice reduces the exposure to blue light emitted by screens, which is known to disrupt sleep patterns and can exacerbate anxiety.

Weekends or specific times of day can also become tech-free. Perhaps Sunday afternoons are reserved for outdoor activities, hobby time, or simply lounging with a book. During these periods, you're not merely avoiding technology; you're replacing it with activities that feed your soul and reduce anxiety.

For families with children, these routines provide an excellent framework for teaching balance and the value of personal interaction. Involve children in the process by creating tech-free family activities that everyone can look forward to, such as game nights, cooking together, or exploring nature.

Enforcing these tech-free times may be challenging, especially in the beginning. However, with consistency and commitment, the household will adapt. When people experience the refreshment that comes from unplugging, the initial resistance will likely dissolve into appreciation.

Don't forget to communicate your intentions. Share with your household why these tech-free zones and routines are being established. Understanding the why can be a powerful motivator for adherence. When everyone is on board with the goal of decreased anxiety and increased mental clarity, the transition becomes much easier.

Moreover, address any resistance with patience and encouragement. Remember, the ingrained habits around technology won't vanish overnight. Acknowledge the efforts of both yourself and your household, celebrating successes, no matter how small they may seem.

Be flexible and willing to adapt. Over time, you may find that certain tech-free zones or routines need adjusting. Encourage open dialogue about what's working and what isn't. This ensures that everyone feels heard and that the spaces in your home can genuinely be those of relaxation and calm.

Lastly, lead by example. As you adopt these new habits, your actions will speak volumes. When you reach for a book instead of the remote or engage in meditative practices over scrolling through social media, others will take note. Your behavior can be a powerful catalyst for change within the household.

Incorporating tech-free zones and routines within the household serves as a steadfast approach to reducing anxiety and fostering mental clarity. It's an investment in your well-being and that of your home's inhabitants. By mindfully managing technology's role in your daily life, you create spaces that nurture the mind, soul, and the relationships within them.

Chapter 8:
Maintaining Your Anxiety-Free Abode

As we draw close to the end of our journey toward creating an anxiety-free living environment, it's essential to reflect on the transformative steps we've taken together. You've embraced the challenge of modifying your home and habits to make way for peace and tranquility in your domestic life. This vision of serenity does not end here; instead, it evolves into the practices and rituals that you will maintain going forward.

Think of your home now, not merely as a physical space but as a sanctuary that reflects the harmony within your own mind. You've learned the crucial elements of establishing a calm environment, which is the bedrock for your overall well-being.

As you move on from this point, remember the importance of recognizing and reducing household stressors. The cues you've learned to observe will continue to guide you as your sanctuary evolves with life's inevitable changes.

Consider the regularity of your calming routines and the soothing order you've instilled in your physical environment. Upholding these practices is paramount in maintaining a stable and serene home. Your daily rhythms are now intertwined with mindfulness, and with each mindful moment, you reaffirm your commitment to mental clarity.

Regular decluttering will remain an essential part of your life, not just as a chore but as a form of self-care. The freedom you've gained from the clutter that once burdened you is restoring energy and focus into your life. Sustainability isn't just about what we leave behind for future generations; it's also about sustaining the peace in our own lives day-to-day.

The connections you've nurtured within your home have become stronger and more resilient. These relationships stand as pillars of support in your ongoing effort to create a shared, anxiety-free space. Clear and kind communication has opened doorways to understanding and empathy amongst those you share your home with.

Remember to continue embracing holistic health practices. The natural remedies, the scents of aromatherapy, and the wholesome meals have not only nourished your body but also your soul. They are to be regular fixtures in your abode, elements of a ritual that honors both your health and your happiness.

As technology's pervasive glow dims in your sanctuary, you've reclaimed time and mental space. The balance you've achieved by moderating screen time and creating tech-free zones is delicate and needs your commitment to remain effective.

The culmination of these efforts, these chapters in your life, is the realization of an anxiety-free abode. Yet, a conclusion is simply a new beginning. The peace you've meticulously curated must be actively preserved. It's a conscious choice you make daily, with every thoughtful action and every calm, deep breath you take.

Consider setting aside time each week to review and adjust your strategies for maintaining this peaceful environment. As your life shifts and the world around you changes, so also must your approach to keeping an anxiety-free home. This maintenance is not a set of tasks but a lifestyle that honors the tranquility you so deeply deserve.

Find moments to celebrate the transformation you've undergone. Acknowledging the growth that has taken place will fortify your resolve to continue this journey. You've not only reconstructed your living space; you've reconstructed your mental and emotional framework.

As you leverage the resources for continued growth found in Appendix A, embrace the notion that learning and adaptation are perpetual. There is always more to discover about ourselves, our homes, and the interplay of energies between the two.

And finally, take pride in what you've achieved and the environment you've crafted. It's a testament to your dedication and a beacon of tranquility in a tumultuous world. Your anxiety-free abode isn't just a place; it's a testament to the robust serenity that lies within you.

Walking forward, arm in arm with the practices you've honed, you're more than prepared to sustain the quiet comfort you've built. This isn't the end; it's a way of life. And with each day, you're reaffirming your commitment to a serene and fulfilling home life, free from the chains of anxiety.

So continue to tend to your abode with the same care and attention as a gardener to their beloved plants. It is an ever-growing, living space that thrives on your nurturing. Your anxiety-free abode is not just a dream realized but a legacy you nurture each passing day.

Appendix A:
Resources for Continued Growth

As you embark upon this journey of nurturing mental clarity and alleviating anxiety, remember that growth is a perpetual process. To support your ongoing efforts beyond the strategies and insights shared, it's essential to have a trove of dependable resources. These can serve not just as a means for further learning, but as a wellspring for inspiration and resilience. In this appendix, we've curated a collection of resources aimed at fostering your continuous evolution towards an anxiety-free existence.

Books and Publications

Knowledge is a profound tool for empowerment. Invigorate your mind with literature that deepens your understanding of anxiety and equips you with innovative strategies to ease it. Books such as "The Anxiety and Phobia Workbook" by Edmund J. Bourne offer actionable steps for tackling anxiety, while "10% Happier" by Dan Harris relates a personal quest for peace amidst chaos. Scientific journals and publications in psychology can also provide valuable insights into recent research and advancements in the mental health field.

Online Courses

Step into the world of online learning where courses on personal development, mindfulness, stress management, and more await you.

Platforms like Coursera, Udemy, and Headspace provide access to teachings from top experts. You can work at your own pace, revisit lessons that resonate deeply, and build upon the practices discussed in this book.

Websites and Blogs

There's a plethora of blogs and websites dedicated to mental well-being. Sites like Psych Central, The Mighty, and Tiny Buddha are treasure troves of articles that tackle various aspects of anxiety, from coping mechanisms to personal stories of triumph. These can be both comforting and educative, showcasing that you're not alone in your experiences.

Local Support Groups

Ground your journey in community by connecting with local support groups. Whether through intimate meetups or larger workshops, there's profound strength in shared experiences. These groups offer a safe environment to express concerns, learn from others, and build connections that transcend the sessions themselves.

Professional Counseling

If you're finding yourself in need of more structured support, don't hesitate to seek professional counseling. A therapist can tailor strategies to your unique needs, building upon the foundational work you've already initiated. There are numerous directories like the American Psychological Association's Psychologist Locator to help you find a licensed professional near you.

Apps for Mental Well-being

Technological advancements have made managing anxiety more accessible. Apps such as Calm, Insight Timer, and Breathe2Relax offer functions ranging from guided meditations to stress-tracking features. They can be integrated into your daily routine, providing support and guidance at the touch of a button.

As you continue to forge your path to a more serene and centered life, these resources can become your companions, illuminating new facets of your journey and reinforcing your commitment to mental serenity. Endeavor to explore them, absorb their wisdom, and allow your understanding—and mastery—of personal tranquility to flourish.

www.ingramcontent.com/pod-product-compliance
Lightning Source LLC
Chambersburg PA
CBHW071109260726
48661CB00006B/2548